Working Together

Paul Humphrey

Illustrated by

Hemesh Alles

Evans

I'm trying to build a den.
It's not very easy.

Sometimes it's difficult to do things on your own. Then you have to ask someone for help.

5

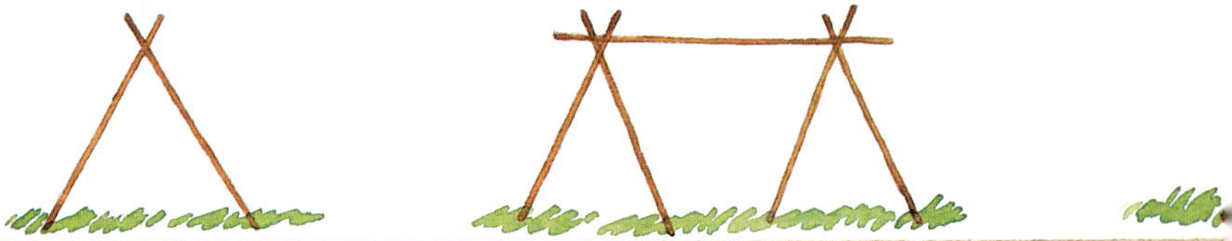

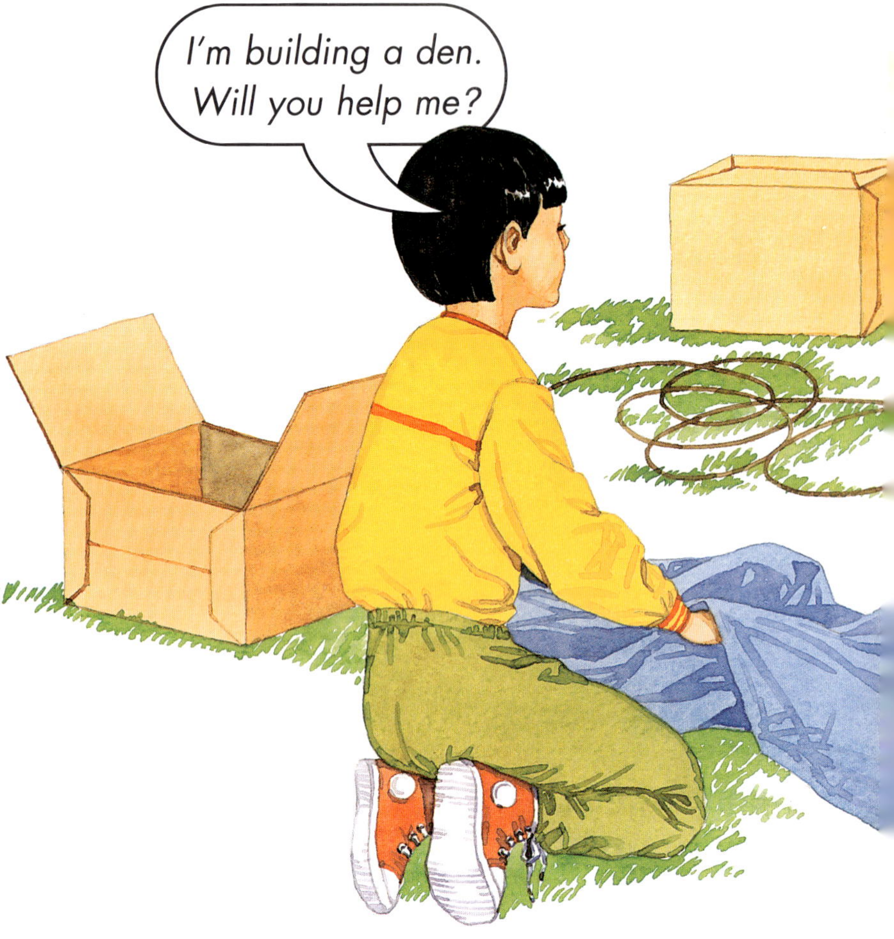
I'm building a den.
Will you help me?

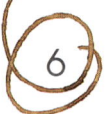

Of course. My friend can help us, too.

It can be much easier to do things if you work together with your friends.

What a terrific den!

I couldn't have made it without your help.

8

We all need help sometimes to get things done.

Let's think of other people who work together.

Fire-fighters work together

10

They have to help each other to put out the fire.

Fire-fighters depend on each other when they are fire-fighting. If one of the team gets into trouble, the others can help.

Climbers have to work together.

Climbers are often roped together for safety. If a climber slips or falls, the other members of the climbing team will pull him or her to safety.

We work together at school.

We help each other in the classroom...

...and with the school concert.

School is a good place to work together. You can do things that you can't do alone. You can perform concerts and plays.

Football players work together.

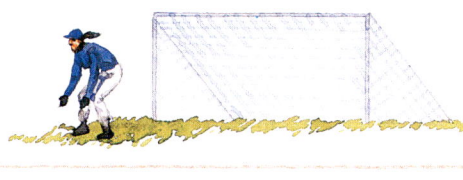

Football players have to practise so that they can play together as a team.

Our family works together.

We all have jobs to do.

Everyone in a family who is old enough has something to do. Parents work together to bring up their children.

Some animals work together.

Wolves live and hunt together in packs. This means they can hunt animals that are larger than themselves. The wolves work together to feed their young.

The bright colours and strong smell of the flowers attract bees. Bees collect nectar from flowers and pick up pollen at the same time.

The bees carry the pollen to other flowers.
The different pollen helps the flowers
to make seeds.

Look at the bee on this flower.

Countries work together.

Countries work together to try to solve problems in the world. The richer countries try to help the poorer countries.

Countries work together to find cures for disease and to save endangered animals.

When people work together they can solve all sorts of problems.

We work together to solve puzzles.

I like working together.

I think we should always work together.

28

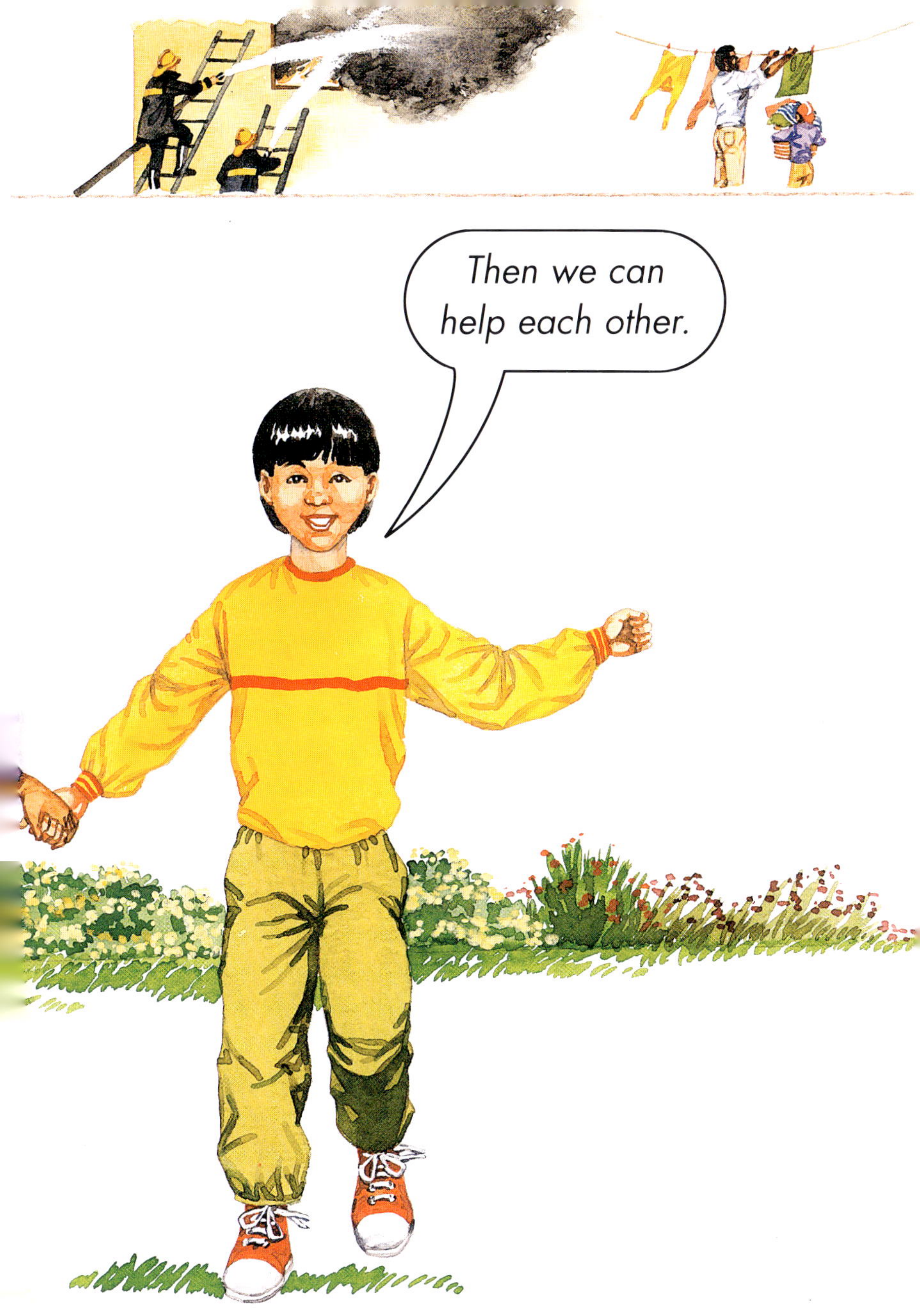
Then we can help each other.

The pictures below show some examples of working and playing together. Let's see if you can remember what they are?